Love Is Forever

A Romantic Ride on Cupid's Arrow

Compiled and Edited
by
Karol Cooper and Alan Ross

WALNUT GROVE PRESS
Nashville, TN 37211

ISBN 1-58334-000-9

In most instances, material for this book was obtained from secondary sources, primarily print media. In all cases, the authors have attempted to maintain the speaker's original intent. While every effort was made to ensure the accuracy of these sources, the accuracy cannot be guaranteed. For additions, deletions, corrections or clarifications in future editions of this text, please write WALNUT GROVE PRESS.

Printed in the United States of America
Cover Design by Tal Howell Design
Typesetting & Page Layout by Sue Gerdes
1 2 3 4 5 6 7 8 9 10 • 99 00 01 02 03 04 05

ACKNOWLEDGMENTS
The authors gratefully acknowledge the friendship, deep support, and opportunity extended by Dr. Criswell Freeman. Special thanks to the magnificent staff at Walnut Grove Press, whose great work makes magical things happen.

Love Is Forever

For our mothers

Wilma Cooper and Helen Ross

who taught us the true meaning of love

Table of Contents

Remembrance

The unerring trajectory of Cupid's arrow pierced both Alan and me when we met at a party in the spring of 1990. We were both reeling from the heartbreak of failed marriages, and neither of us was prepared to be stricken by Eros, that most unyielding of the timeless Greek gods. Nevertheless, as Love persistently insists, we were married in early 1995.

During that ceremony, a precious gem staked its claim for remembrance. Our hard-of-hearing (and now dearly departed) landlord and friend, the venerable Jim G. Brown, sensed a lull in the proceedings when he noticed the preacher and wedding participants standing motionless for minutes on end early in the ceremony. What Mr. Brown could not hear was the back-to-back playing of several prerecorded songs emanating from a small sound system. To everyone's delight, the 87-year-old gentleman then loudly remarked to his nearby daughter, "What do you reckon the holdup is?"

A great day for marriage was blessed with an ample topping of mirth. How could anything be more perfect?

k.c.

Introduction

For all of time, the Moon has played a leading romantic role in Love's urgent scenarios.

Amour has always had its own distinct language. For instance, to be "moonstruck" is to be romantically sentimental (though it also can mean one who is mentally unbalanced. And who of us, caught in its throes, has not come delightfully unhinged from the experience of it!). The phrase "honeymoon," historically, refers to the sweet month after the marriage, while tributes to the Moon in song have been rendered both meaningfully tender and overly dramatic by every songwriter who's ever been touched by its mysterious beams. From "Blue Moon" to "Moon River," over 4,400 licensed songs exist that honor our lunar sphere as the light of Love.

When contemplating Love, there is little need to mince words. All the great poets, thinkers, and romantics have already gloriously expressed this rapturous state in the most eloquent of terms.

In this edition, we attempt to present a mix of some of the best of Love's purveyors, from Cupid to the Kama Sutra, from Lawrence to Lewis, from Byron to Baudelaire, and all the great romantics in between.

Our wish for all is that you may know Love and its many forms intimately. And better, may you revel in it under a waxing crescent Moon.

A.R.

At the touch of love,
everyone becomes
a poet.

Plato

Chapter 1

A Thing Called Love

Love's myriad looks resemble a garden of bountiful color and variety — a fine mist of infinite droplets, each with its own distinct hue and character.

The cumulative grains of sand on all the beaches of the world probably don't outnumber the singularly unique appearances of love.

Herein lies a varied collection of some of Love's many voices, imparting their own viewpoints on the one topic that makes our world and life itself go around: that crazy little thing called Love.

Love is an irresistible desire
    to be irresistibly desired.

Robert Frost

Love can turn the cottage
    into a golden palace.

German proverb

Love is too vast and elusive to deal with
    as a whole.

Arthur D. Colman
Libby Lee Colman

Of all important human words it has been used, and abused, in more varied senses than any other. It can describe a range of behaviour from sanctity to Sade…

Rosemary Haughton

Nobody knows or will ever know everything they need to know about love. Anyone who says they fully understand love is either lying, stupid or dead.

Robert Fulghum

I wonder why love is so often
equated with joy, when it is
everything else as well —
devastation, balm, obsession,
granting and receiving excessive
value, and losing it again.
It is recognition, often, of what
you are not, but might be.
It sears and heals.
It is beyond pity and above law.
It can seem like truth.

Florida Scott-Maxwell

A Thing Called Love

Half the love songs and half the love poems
in the world will tell you that the Beloved
is your fate or destiny, no more your choice
than a thunderbolt....

C.S. Lewis

The unity of love is more like the
responsiveness between violin and piano in a
Mozart sonata or the concerted rhythm of
paddlers in a canoe.

Irving Singer

To say the word Romanticism is to say
modern art — that is, intimacy, spirituality,
color, aspiration towards the infinite,
expressed by every means available
to the arts.

Charles Baudelaire

Sure this is love, which heretofore
I conceived to be the dream of idle maids
and wanton poets.

Dr. Samuel Johnson

Gravitation cannot be held responsible for people falling in love.

Albert Einstein

The relationship of love to behavior is complex: I mean we cannot describe what it is like for a man to be loving as easily as we can describe what it is like for a man to be walking.

Herbert McCabe

Being with you is like walking on a very clear morning — definitely the sensation of belonging there.

E.B. White

Love itself is "bigger" than those it
embraces, serves, lifts up and transforms.

Rosemary Haughton

Lovers choose each other for the sense
of excitement or completion they experience
together. They do not necessarily see
themselves as equals.

Arthur D. Colman
Libby Lee Colman

There is indeed a peculiar charm...about
those moments when Appreciative love lies
curled up asleep, and the mere ease and
ordinariness of the relationship...wraps us
round. No need to talk. No need to make love.
No needs at all except perhaps to stir the fire.

C.S. Lewis

Somewhere there's someone who dreams of your smile, and finds in your presence that life is worth while, so when you are lonely, remember this is true: Somebody, somewhere is thinking of you.

Unknown

Love is essentially tenderness between
the male and the female and therefore sacred
to the human sensibility.

Mulk Raj Anand

Love is the basic passion of man.
Every emotion of the heart is reducible to it.

Bishop Fulton J. Sheen

Love has a constant quality which, when
pointed out, can be recognized anywhere....
It can overcome all the ingenious methods
devised by the human fear of it.

Rosemary Haughton

For most of us, love is a preoccupation
that we never outgrow.

Irving Singer

When you love someone, all your saved-up
wishes start coming out.

Elizabeth Bowen

Love is reveling in humanness.

Arthur D. Colman
Libby Lee Colman

Eros will have naked bodies;
Friendship naked personalities.

C.S. Lewis

I am you and you are love and that is
what makes the world go 'round.

Clive Barker

Perfect love is to feeling what perfect white
is to color. Many think that white is the
absence of color. It is not. It is the inclusion
of all color....So, too, love is not the absence
of an emotion (hatred, anger, lust, jealousy,
covetousness), but the summation of all
feeling. It is the sum total.
The everything.

Neale Donald Walsch

All mankind loves a lover.

Ralph Waldo Emerson

The loving are the daring.

Bayard Taylor

Men always want to be a woman's first love.
Women have a more subtle instinct:
What they like is to be a man's last romance.

Oscar Wilde

All love is sweet, given or returned.

Percy Bysshe Shelley

Love makes up for the lack of long memories
by a sort of magic. All other affections need
a past; love creates a past which envelops us
as if by enchantment.

Benjamin Constant de Rebecque

O happy hours when I may once more
encircle within these arms the dearest object
of my love — when I shall again feel the
pressure of that "aching head" which will
delight to recline upon my bosom, when I may
again press to my heart which palpitates with
the purest affection that loved one who has
so long shared its undivided emotion.

Alexander Hamilton Rice

Love is not merely a contributor
to meaningful life. In its own way it may
underlie all other forms of meaning.

Irving Singer

Love is a reaching out towards something
further and deeper in human life.

Rosemary Haughton

Love is the most basic human need, at the
level of life at which human beings are able
to be human, because their energies are not
entirely absorbed by the need to keep alive.

Rosemary Haughton

At the beginning and at the end of love,
the two lovers are embarrassed to find
themselves alone.

La Bruyere

Fantasy love is much better than reality love.
The most exciting attractions are between
two opposites that never meet.

Andy Warhol

Love is the river of life in this world. Think not that ye know it who stand at the little tinkling rill, the first small fountain. Not until you have gone through the rocky gorges, and not lost the stream; not until you have gone through the meadow, and the stream has widened and deepened until fleets could ride on its bosom; not until beyond the meadow you have come to the unfathomable ocean, and poured your treasures into its depths — not until then can you know what love is.

Henry Ward Beecher

I may not be a smart man but I know what love is.

Forrest Gump

Aphrodite, the goddess of love, wore a
magic girdle which caused those who saw
her to fall immediately in love with her…
She tempted men and women alike into her
bed of roses…A fleet of cupids obeyed her
orders and traveled to the world of humans
and, by shooting arrows into their hearts,
made men and women fall in love
with one another.

Manuela Dunn Mascetti

Chapter 2

Cupid's Arrow

Everyone from Buddy Holly to Connie Francis to Vanilla Ice has sung about the magical little nymph-god who, if he cared at all, could probably be the perennial quadrennial Olympic gold medalist in Archery. For Cupid's aim, if not occasionally surprising, is ever true and on the mark.

Now, out of the quiver, onto the bow; prepare for a ride on Love's arrow!

And Psyche, gazing hungrily thereon, draws an arrow from the quiver, and trying the point upon her thumb, tremulous still, drave in the barb, so that a drop of blood came forth. Thus fell she, by her own act, and unaware, into the love of Love.

Lucius Apuleius,
trans. Walter Pater,
Marius the Epicurean

Cupid's Arrow

It is the sign of a noble heart when
a young man burns with a flame of love.

Italian proverb

Love finds its way round corners and
through underground passages and emerges,
somehow, somewhere, though usually
with little acclaim.

Rosemary Haughton

The brain's addiction to arousal clouds our
consciousness and destroys our rationality,
resulting in our submission to cuteness and
coitus rather than caring and cognition....
"Cupid makes you stupid."

Paul Pearsall

The sheer force of love remains astonishing...
Cupid and Psyche, Tristan and Isolde,
Romeo and Juliet, Tony and Maria of West
Side Story — the doomed lovers —
are the salvation of the hard-hearted.

Rosemary Haughton

Very often what comes first is simply a delighted pre-occupation with the Beloved... in her totality. A man in this state really hasn't leisure to think of sex. He is too busy thinking of a person....He is full of desire, but the desire may not be sexually toned. If you asked him what he wanted, the true reply would often be, "To go on thinking of her." He is love's contemplative.

C.S. Lewis

Yes, I now feel that it was then on that evening of sweet dreams — that the very first dawn of human love burst upon the icy night of my spirit. Since that period I have never seen nor heard your name without a shiver half of delight, half of anxiety...For years your name never passed my lips, while my soul drank in, with a delirious thirst, all that was uttered in my presence respecting you.

Edgar Allan Poe

We always remember the first time with a lover.

Manuela Dunn Mascetti

All that is in the heart is written on the face.

Proverb

The language of love is in the eyes.

Italian proverb

The soul that can speak through the eyes
can also kiss with a gaze.

Unknown

The sound of a kiss is not as strong
as that of a cannon, but its echo may endure
much longer.

Italian proverb

In Eros at times we seem to be flying;
　　Venus gives us the sudden twitch that
reminds us we are really captive balloons.

C.S. Lewis

Though people describe their experience of
falling in love as if it were a bolt from the blue,
this tempestuous event is the outcome of a
destiny they have chosen for themselves.

Irving Singer

Follow your heart because your heart
　　will know the love that is meant for you.

Unknown

We must know that love is the flame
　　of life and makes time worthwhile.

Italian proverb

I fell in love with her courage, her sincerity, and her flaming self-respect and it's these things I'd believe in even if the whole world indulged in wild suspicions that she wasn't all she should be... I love her and that's the beginning of everything.

F. Scott Fitzgerald

Lovers commune with each other's souls
but not with each other's whims, emotions,
anxieties, and peculiarities. They incredibly
overvalue each other.

Arthur D. Colman
Libby Lee Colman

Love makes vows unasked...
"I will be ever true," are almost the first words
he utters. Not hypocritically but sincerely.
No experience will cure him of the delusion.

C.S. Lewis

When we find someone whose weirdness
is compatible with ours, we join up with them
and fall into mutually satisfying weirdness —
and call it love — true love.

Robert Fulghum

Many a lover idealizes his beloved
to the point of worship.

Arthur D. Colman
Libby Lee Colman

. . . I wish I had the gift of making rhymes,
for methinks there is poetry in my head
and heart since I have been in love with you.
You are a poem.

Nathaniel Hawthorne,
to Sophia Peabody

I cannot exist without you. I am forgetful of everything but seeing you again — my life seems to stop there — I can see no further. You have absorbed me. I have a sensation at the present moment as though I were dissolving…I have been astonished that Men could die Martyrs for religion — I have shuddered at it — I shudder no more. I could be martyred for my Religion: Love is my religion. I could die for that. I could die for you. My creed is Love and you are its only tenet. You have ravished me away by a Power I cannot resist.

John Keats

Your words are my food, your breath my wine. You are everything to me.

Sarah Bernhardt

Eros wants the Beloved.

C.S. Lewis

If I know what love is,
it is because of you.

Herman Hesse

Cupid's Arrow

What looks like a seizure from without —
the innocent and hapless individual suddenly
struck by an arrow from Cupid's bow —
may be taken as a manifestation of meaning
being created in accordance with whatever
needs or desires the lover accepts
as paramount at the moment.

Irving Singer

Love distills desire upon the eyes,
love brings bewitching grace into the heart.

Euripides

It is the very mark of Eros that when he is in
us we had rather share unhappiness with the
Beloved than be happy on any other terms....
Even when it becomes clear beyond evasion
that marriage with the Beloved cannot
possibly lead to happiness — when it cannot
even profess to offer any other life than that of
tending an incurable invalid, of hopeless
poverty, of exile, or of disgrace — Eros never
hesitates to say, "Better this than parting.
Better to be miserable with her than
happy without her."

C.S. Lewis

Love is...born with the pleasure of looking at each other, it is fed with the necessity of seeing each other, it is concluded with the impossibility of separation.

Jose Marti y Perez

Love is called blind because the lover can refuse to see the unlovely aspects of his beloved. The beloved is like a deity, fixed and immutable.

Arthur D. Colman
Libby Lee Colman

The hours I spend with you I look upon as a sort of perfumed garden, a dim twilight, and a fountain singing to it...you and you alone make me feel that I am alive...Other men it is said have seen angels, but I have seen thee and thou art enough.

George Moore

The way you let your hand rest in mine,
my bewitching Sweetheart, fills me with
happiness. It is the perfection of confiding love.
Everything you do, the little unconscious
things in particular, charms me and increases
my sense of nearness to you, identification with
you, till my heart is full to overflowing.

Woodrow Wilson

Two souls with but a single thought,
two hearts that beat as one.

John Keats

And what's romance? Usually, a nice little tale where you have everything As You Like It, where rain never wets your jacket and gnats never bite your nose and it's always daisy-time.

D.H. Lawrence

The heights of most love ecstasies occur
when contact is still on a fantasy level.
Arthur D. Colman
Libby Lee Colman

In one sense we are disqualified from
understanding what is really happening
when we ourselves are involved
in an ardent relationship.
Irving Singer

We think of love as something that just
happens, as "made in heaven" or as
"chemistry," implying it is magical and out
of control. We rarely think of love as something requiring work or discipline.
Arthur D. Colman
Libby Lee Colman

Eros makes a man really want, not a woman,
but one particular woman.

C.S. Lewis

She walks in Beauty, like the night
Of cloudless climes and starry skies,
And all that's best of dark and bright
Meet in her aspect and her eyes.

Lord Byron

But to see her was to love her,
and love her forever.

Robert Burns

My heart was already fattening up at the sight of him.

Joyce Carol Oates

Put aside thy woe, and turn thy prayers to Cupid. He is in truth a delicate youth: win him by the delicacy of thy service.

Lucius Apuleius,
trans. Walter Pater,
Marius the Epicurean

Pains of love be sweeter
far than all other
pleasures are.

John Dryden

Chapter 3

Love Hurts

How can something that feels so good, hurt so bad!? Love's premier paradox takes center stage, with a poking probe and some curious commentary from those who have fallen victim to the inexplicable dichotomy of romantic love.

Paramedics stand by the ready. And while you're at it, better break out the Band-Aids and smelling salts.

Ever has it been that love knows not its own
depth until the hour of separation.

Kahlil Gibran,
The Prophet

Where love is, pain is never far away....
Every love story has an unhappy ending,
sooner or later — even if love lasts a lifetime,
somebody dies first, leaving somebody
behind with the pain of grief.

Robert Fulghum

Who doubts that the lover can find
happiness in his beloved? But it is no less
certain that love is sometimes sad, as sad
as death — a supreme and mortal torment.

José Ortega y Gasset

Their meetings made December June,
  Their every parting was to die.
Alfred, Lord Tennyson

When love goes, it is as if the sun itself had
stopped shining. One is used to living, walking,
talking, thinking, eating, sleeping, working,
laughing and crying with the other. When the
other is no longer there, a major psychological
shift needs to occur in order to return
to aloneness.
Manuela Dunn Mascetti

I wish she only knew of my desires,
  So that, without speaking, she should show,
  Pity on me for the torments that I suffer.
Guido Guinizelli,
trans. Richard A. Branyon

One must learn to love and go through a
good deal of suffering to get to it…and the
journey is always towards the other soul….
D.H. Lawrence

The terrible conflicts of truly loving people
are a witness to the ruthless demand that
love makes on people who allow themselves
to listen.
Rosemary Haughton

Let me still love you and look on you
And sign for you, since
Sadness, weeping and sorrow are
The only rewards I have for my love.
Torquato Tasso,
trans. Richard A. Branyon

Love is a pervasive interpenetration that
not only causes each person to care about the
other but also to reject, and frequently to
dread, the possibility of life without the other.

Irving Singer

If Affection is made the absolute sovereign of
a human life the seeds will germinate. Love,
having become a god, becomes a demon.

C.S. Lewis

Love is a sweet tyranny, because the lover
endures his torment willingly.

Unknown

The wound that Love has dealt the lord
Won't heal like wounds from lance or sword,
For any wound a sword has cut
The doctors can cure quickly, but
The wounds of Love, by definition,
Are worst when nearest their physician.

Chretien de Troyes, Yvaine,
or The Knight with the Lion,
trans. Ruth Harwood Cline

In secret we met In silence I grieve
That thy heart could forget Thy spirit deceive.
If I should meet thee after long years,
How should I greet thee?
With silence and tears.

Lord Byron

Unrequited love arouses desperation.
Such feelings shouldn't be dismissed as the
cute foolishness of a child. Such feelings are
the heart and soul of great literature,
high tragedy, and grand opera.

Robert Fulghum

. . . the pain and suffering of unrequited
love was more sublime than the physical
pleasures and harmony of love fulfilled.

Arthur D. Colman
Libby Lee Colman

But how does anyone who doesn't experience it know what is sickness and what is well-being? Mine is different from all other illnesses, for to tell you the truth, it pleases me greatly and yet I suffer from it, and I find delight in my discomfort. And if what pleases can be a sickness, then my trouble is what I want, and my suffering my health....I feel so well in my desire that it makes me suffer sweetly, and I find so much joy in my trouble that I'm pleasantly ill...There's nothing to be afraid of: I'll readily tell you both the nature of your sickness.

Chretien de Troyes, Cliges,
in Arthurian Romances,
trans. D. D. R. Owen

Love, being jealous, makes a good eye
look asquint.

Unknown

Heavens above! The reason why I'm so
jealous of you is obvious enough! If you
weren't so attractive physically, do you think
my heart would beat almost to suffocation
whenever I see you speak to someone?

Violet Trefussis

The essence of romantic love is that
wonderful beginning, after which sadness and
impossibility may become the rule.

Anita Brookner

Love is a confection of the mind,
a sugary fable, and potentially dangerous.

Irving Singer

'Tis better to have loved and lost
than never to have loved at all.

Alfred, Lord Tennyson

My incomparable Josephine, away from
you there is no happiness. Away from you
the world is a desert.

Napoleon Bonaparte

The choice between accepting ourselves
as self-sufficient and reaching out to another
is an eternal conflict...It is as difficult to be
alone as it is to be intimate.

Arthur D. Colman
Libby Lee Colman

I do not know how to part with what I am not tired with.

Hon. Charles Francis Greville,
on Edith Hamilton

Ooooh, love hurts!

Alice Cooper

Love is the healer, the
reconciler, the inspirer,
the creator...

Rosemary Haughton

Chapter 4

Love Heals

Love is the great healer. Those of us who have known a rich and satisfying relationship with our mate can attest to that. Love reaches down into the deepest, darkest pit of the soul and plants flowers of hope and health. And Love is the light that causes those flowers to grow and bloom.

Love's most profound healing power is exercised when we love unconditionally, when we accept our mate with all his or her idiosyncrasies, kinks and twists of personality. That's when Love speaks to the deepest part of us and says, "You are worthy." By fully loving our lovers, we bring divine healing into the world.

To love is to receive
a glimpse of heaven.

Karen Sunde

And indeed I felt happy with her,
so perfectly happy that the one desire of mine
was that it should differ in nothing from hers,
and already I wished for nothing beyond her
smile, and to walk with her thus, hand in hand,
along a sun-warmed, flower-bordered path.

Andre Gide

First, to be able to love, then to learn
that body and spirit are one.

Hugo von Hofmannsthal

The human need to love is infinitely adaptable.

Rosemary Haughton

Healing by forgiving ourselves and others
is necessity within partnership.
Richard and Carole Runyeon

Emotional healing is an ongoing process.
We move through it layer by layer, sometimes
gently, sometimes intensely. Everyone is
different, and we each have our own rhythm
and timing.
Shakti Gawain

Love may not really make
the world go around, but
you can often get around
in the world with love.

Robert Fulghum

Friendship alone, of all the loves, seems
   to raise you to the level of gods or angels.

C.S. Lewis

Friendship at first sight, like love at first sight,
   is said to be the only truth.

Herman Melville

Do not try to beat evil with more evil —
it doesn't work. But you can destroy evil
with love.

Paul of Tarsus

Love is something so positive, so strong,
so real, that it is as impossible for one who
loves to take back that feeling as it is to take
his own life.

Vincent van Gogh

Being deeply loved by someone gives you
strength, while loving someone deeply
gives you courage.

Lao-tzu

Love means never having to say you're sorry.

Erich Segal
from the movie Love Story

Love conquers all except poverty and toothaches.

Mae West

All you need is love.

John Lennon

All love takes time
to develop. It is never
something that
just happens.

Irving Singer

Chapter 5

Keeping Love Alive

Twenty years ago I listened as Pastor Millard Reed expressed from the pulpit his disgust and dismay at the divorce rate, particularly within the church. He said, "If you aren't in love with your spouse anymore then you'd better get busy!" That message stuck, and I've come to believe that we build our romantic health one day at a time. A soft-spoken word, an understanding response, a listening ear, help with the chores, a well-placed hug — all these small daily acts build the bedrock on which we fashion our love.

To paraphrase Edgar A. Guest, it takes a heap 'o lovin' in a house t' make it home. Be pro-active in love. Give your lover a back massage. Read passages of this book to each other. Curl up together by candlelight and whisper sweet nothings. Dream together. Together you can give your love the food it needs.

Get busy falling in love!

Love does not arise
spontaneously, it arises
in response to
something else.

Rosemary Haughton

A gentle heart always returns love,
  As a tall tree gives shade to the grass.
                                    Italian proverb

Beloved, all that is harsh and difficult
  I want for myself, and all that is gentle
    and sweet for thee.
                                San Juan de la Cruz

The leaf when loved becomes a flower,
  The flower when loved becomes a fruit.
                                    Italian proverb

There is only one happiness in life,
    to love and be loved.
                                    George Sand

Love is an active verb —
a river, not a pond.

Robert Fulghum

Top Ten Tips for a Good Relationship

1. Call if you're going to be late.
2. Disagree without being disagreeable.
3. The harsher the truth, the gentler you tell it.
4. Encouragement works. Nagging doesn't.
5. A goodbye kiss — don't leave home without it.
6. You never outgrow your need for hugs.
7. Good listeners make the best lovers.
8. You keep a lifetime commitment by keeping promises day by day.
9. Warm your feet before you climb into bed.
10. If you like Italian and she likes Mexican, order taco pizza.

We reserve the right to
serve only those in love,
those who have been in
love, or those who want
to be in love.

Sign in a Sicilian restaurant

A woman would run through fire and water
for such a kind heart.

William Shakespeare

In her eyes, my lady carries love and
makes gentle everything that she looks upon.

Italian proverb

When a man is a good listener, a woman
can repeatedly find the place in her heart that
is capable of loving him and embracing him
just the way he is.

John Gray

A Heart's Friend

Fair is the white star of twilight,
And the sky clearer at the days end;
But she is fairer and she is dearer
She, my heart's friend.

Fair is the white star of twilight,
And the moon roving to the sky's end;
But she is fairer, better worth loving
She, my heart's friend.

Shoshone Love Song

Love's musical instrument is as old, and as poor, as a penny-whistle: it has but two stops; and yet, you see, the cunning musician does thus much with it!

George Meredith,
The Ordeal of Richard Feverel

What's the difference between the music of my generation and today's? Our songs were about Love and Romance, today's music is chiefly about sex; which I might add gets a little boring.

David A. Vigilanti

If spouses celebrate and renew their love
through sentimental remembrances of their
original ardor, or through anniversary
dinners, or second and third honeymoons,
they do so not because they want to bring
back the emotional turmoil of falling in love,
but rather because they cherish the
romantic element that was present in it.

Irving Singer

Love peaks and then passes. Rarely can it be continuously experienced, for the traffic of our daily lives distracts us from the ecstasy of our relationship with another.

Arthur D. Colman
Libby Lee Colman

She who makes her husband and her children happy, who reclaims the one from vice and trains up the other to virtue, is a much greater character than the ladies described in romance, whose whole occupation is to murder mankind with shafts from their quiver or their eyes.

Joan Oliver Goldsmith

Sometimes I wonder if men and women really suit each other. Perhaps they should live next door and just visit now and then.

Katharine Hepburn

Ideally, couples need three lives: one for him, one for her, and one for them together.

Jacqueline Bisset

Couples who play together stay together.

Paul Pearsall

Tenderness and kindness are not signs of weakness and despair but manifestations of strength and resolution.

Kahlil Gibran

Let your love be genuine, reject what is against love, take good hold of what assists it.

Paul of Tarsus

The phrase I love you expresses
both an accomplished desire and an ongoing
willingness to enter into whatever behavior
will be necessary for love to survive
and to flourish.

Irving Singer

I like not only to be loved,
but to be told I am loved.

George Eliot

Ten Ways to Say "I Love You"

French	*Je t'aime*
German	*Ich liebe Dich*
Italian	*ti amo*
Afrikaans	*Ek het jou liefe*
Scot Gaelic	*Tha gradh agam ort*
Hebrew	*Ani ohev otach*
Navaho	*Ayor anosh'ni*
Japanese	*Kimi o ai shiteru*
Pig Latin	*Ie Ovele Ouye*
Pakistani	*Mujhe Tumse Muhabbat Hai*

Eros, like a godparent,
makes the vows; it is we
who must keep them....
We must do the work
of Eros when Eros is
not present. This all
good lovers know...

C.S. Lewis

There are never enough
"I love yous."

Lenny Bruce

Never let your
willingness grow dim,
let the spirit of love light
up your whole life, as you
hold yourselves at
the service of love.

Paul of Tarsus

Chapter 6

Real Commitment

Putting the "Us" in Trust

We hear the term "commitment" bandied around in all circles, from church to popular magazines. Webster defines it as "a pledge to do something in the future." In today's disposable world, the closest thing we find to true commitment is a mother's love for her child: a love that never quits, never fades, never loses hope.

How powerful our romantic relationships would be if we would only add that vital ingredient: the "tough it out" attitude, a love that won't give up.

Hearts are not had as a gift
           but hearts are earned…
William Butler Yeats

Without respect, love cannot go far.
Alexandre Dumas (père)

The more I give to thee, the more I have,
           for both are infinite.
William Shakespeare,
Juliet to Romeo,
Romeo and Juliet

If equal affection cannot be,
           let the more loving be me.
W.H. Auden

The deepest need of man...is the need
to overcome his separateness, to leave
the prison of his aloneness.

Erich Fromm

Love alone is capable of uniting living beings
in such a way as to complete and fulfill them,
for it alone takes them and joins them by what
is deepest in themselves.

Pierre Teilhard de Chardin

Grow old with me! The best is yet to be.

Robert Browning,
to Elizabeth Barrett Browning

. . . Faith involves a leap.

Vincent Brümmer

. . . How difficult sheer surrender is. Many human beings long for friendship and love, and in this they basically long for surrender of themselves, in which their being is to be fulfilled. Yet they are incapable of taking the decision of unreserved surrender in the encounters of life, or of trusting simply, without being able to hold on to a support, without a guarantee. Many a friendship and many a marriage is wrecked by man's inability to win this victory over himself.

Rudolf Bultmann

I put my trust in you to bestow your love
on me and not in my own capacity to earn
or extort your love from you.

Vincent Brümmer

The man who wants to be loved does not
desire the enslavement of the beloved.

Jean-Paul Sartre

The best proof of love is trust.

Dr. Joyce Brothers

The strongest evidence of love is sacrifice.

Carolyn Fry

Where love is, there is faith.
Where there is no trust, there is no love.
Ellen Royals

The sincerity of the commitments are tested
by the faithfulness of the lover.
Vincent Brümmer

Love requires trust in the fidelity of another.
It is like meditating on an unfixed point,
a pattern which may move or change
or disintegrate at any moment.
Arthur D. Colman
Libby Lee Colman

Depth has one address: fidelity in love.
Dr. Laura

What I do and what I dream include thee,
as the wine must taste of its own grapes.
Elizabeth Barrett Browning

I have spread my dreams under your feet;
Tread softly because you tread
on my dreams.
William Butler Yeats

To love is to place our happiness in the
happiness of another.
Gottfried Wilhem Von Leibniz

Love is that condition in which the happiness
of another person is essential to your own.
Robert A. Heinlein
Stranger in a Strange Land

I ask of you neither eternal love nor fidelity,
but only truth, utter honesty.

Napoleon,
to Josephine

Mutual vulnerability is one of the great gifts
of love: giving the other sufficient emotional
space in which to live and express their soul,
with its reasonable and unreasonable ways,
and then to risk revealing your own soul,
complete with its own absurdities.

Thomas Moore

There's only one thing greater than my fear —
that is my love. My love will always conquer
my fear — but it can't do it immediately.
It needs the full force of my love to do it
and it takes days for that to emerge out
of its dark hiding places.

John Middleton Murry

Merger with a single Other is frightening
for many individuals. It requires trust of oneself
and the Other.

Arthur D. Colman
Libby Lee Colman

To fear love is to fear life.

Bertrand Russell

Love is Forever

Love has a tendency to grow with time,
while desire has a tendency to wither,
and eventually desire is replaced by love
based in trust and companionship.

Vincent Brümmer

Sexual emotions are passing states whereas
a loving relationship involves lasting
commitments.

Vincent Brümmer

When John says to Mary: "I love you",
this is not merely an expression of his feelings
toward her and of the commitments to which
they give rise, but also a plea that she should
reciprocate these feelings and commitments.
Love wants to be returned…

Vincent Brümmer

One can only obey the great law of the heart
that says, "As long as you live, love one
another and take the consequences."

Robert Fulghum

For what is love itself for the one we love best?
An enfolding of immeasurable cares which yet
are better than any joys outside our love.

George Eliot

Oh, what good will writing do?
I want to put my hand out and touch you.
I want to do for you and care for you.
I want to be there when you're sick
and when you're lonesome.

Edith Wharton

My heart is ever at your service.

William Shakespeare

Ye are my Blood
of my Blood,
And Bone of my Bone.
I give ye my Body,
That we Two
might be One,
I give ye my Spirit,
'Til our Life shall be Done.

Scottish Blood Vow

A soulmate is someone who has the locks
to fit our keys, and the keys to fit our
locks. When we feel safe enough to open
the locks, our truest selves step out and
we can be completely and honestly who we
are; we can be loved for who we are and
not for who we're pretending to be.
Our soulmate is the one who makes life
come to life.

Richard Bach

I did love him, alas too tenderly.
We lived together on such terms as man and
wife ought to live, placing perfect confidence
in each other, bearing one another's burdens
and making due allowances
for human imperfection.

Sarah Ripley Stearns

A good marriage is like an oriental rug,
with all those patterns in it.

Helen Fisher,
anthropologist

Choose your love,
      and then love your choice.

Unknown

Love that is not freely given is not love at all.

Vincent Brümmer

Love sought is good, but given unsought
      is better.

William Shakespeare

For those who loved should always feel
      that their love given was love well taken.

Fran White

One of the first things Eros does is
to obliterate the distinction between giving
      and receiving.

C.S. Lewis

The fact that love is necessarily free
does not entail that it is uncommitted.

Vincent Brümmer

All ecstatic traditions require an enduring
commitment. Love is no exception.

Arthur D. Colman
Libby Lee Colman

The hope for permanent oneness
is at the heart of romantic love.

Irving Singer

Both of us are groping and a little lost.
But we are together.

Anne Morrow Lindbergh

Love you?
I am you.

C.S. Lewis

Every love has its art
of love.

C.S. Lewis

Chapter 7

The Art of Lovemaking

Nothing so fires the mind and senses as sex. From its almost overwhelming turbulence upon first initiation to the profound, mystic depths of maturer love, sexual energy has stamped its imprint on life in more ways than simple procreation.

Sometimes sex rules like an imperious leader, taking the head and heart along with it on a sizzling roller coaster ride. Other times, it can open doorways to higher levels of perception and consciousness.

Behind the closed bedroom door lies the prospect of romantic interlude and the pleasurable assurance that two people truly were made for each other. Long may the fires burn.

Sex includes the whole
spectrum of human
emotion and experience;
it is fun, it is play, it is
love, it is learning, it is
prayer, it is meditation,
it is spiritual.

Manuela Dunn Mascetti

The giving and receiving of pleasure is a need
and an ecstasy.

Kahlil Gibran

Love craves the merging of selves.

Robert C. Solomon

Come live with me, and be my love,
And we will some new pleasures prove...

John Donne

Only one answer will take care
of all our questions.

Ingrid Bergman,
Casablanca

The origin of desire is thought.

Catherine Osborne

The source of sexual power is curiosity,
and passion.

Anaïs Nin

The more physical the love, the more sublime.

Italian proverb

Under the sign of Eros we experience flesh
as in itself a beauty to behold.

Irving Singer

Only the united beat of sex and heart
together can create ecstasy.

Anaïs Nin

Sexual love — not just sex — is an ennobling
and spiritually important experience, whereas
lust is just about the opposite.

Rosemary Haughton

Romantic love rejected lust, in or out
of marriage, as the enemy of "true" love.

Rosemary Haughton

There resides a great mystery in everything
erotic, as there is in gravity itself…The erotic
may constantly elude the probing of our
intellect. In our attempts to understand
or appreciate it, we may not get much beyond
a sense of wonderment.

Irving Singer

Make me immortal with a kiss.

Christopher Marlowe,
Dr. Faustus to Helen of Troy

O repeated embraces,
that bind ... with so many
twines that the ivy or
acanthus have no more.
O dew, in which
I bathe and soften my
burnt heart.

Ludovico Ariosto,
Trans. George R. Kay

Women's hemlines were an inch
  above the ground, men were excited by
the shape and mere appearance of an ankle.
Irving Singer

Women can resist a man's love, a man's
  fame, a man's personal appearance, and a
man's money; but they cannot resist a man's
tongue, when he knows how to talk with them.
Wilkie Collins,
The Woman in White, The Second Epoch,
The Story Continued
by Marian Halcombe

Women...have never separated sex
  from feeling, from love of the whole man.
Anaïs Nin

Without Eros none of us would have been
  begotten and without Affection none of us
would have been reared.
C.S. Lewis

Married sex is not only a possible setting
for a truly spiritual love, but also
the most likely one.

Rosemary Haughton

In the act of love we are not merely
ourselves....It is here no impoverishment but
an enrichment to be aware that forces older
and less personal than we work through us.
In us all the masculinity and femininity of the
world, all that is assailant and responsive,
are momentarily focused.

C.S. Lewis

The gliding of the moon through a sky it dimly
illuminates may symbolize our persistent
though gently muted sexual longing.

Irving Singer

Love is blinding.
That is why lovers
like to touch.

German Proverb

The romantic includes within itself
a longing for integration with the libidinal and
the erotic.

Irving Singer

Intellectual, imaginative, romantic, emotional.
This is what gives sex its surprising textures,
its subtle transformations....

Anaïs Nin

Love is the only game not called on account
of darkness.

Anonymous

Sexual emotion is just as sexual
when unsatisfied.

Rosemary Haughton

Take my breath away.

William Shakespeare,
Marc Antony to Cleopatra,
Antony and Cleopatra

And we are put on earth
a little space
That we may learn to bear
the beams of love.

William Blake

Chapter 8

Love During Difficult Times

When my oldest son was 18 years old and had been playing in the same band for several years, the members began fighting among themselves. I asked him if he thought the band would break up, and in his youthful wisdom he replied, "Being in a band is like being married. When times get tough, you just grit your teeth and get through it."

Out of the mouths of babes…

Bearing the beams of love is not easy — often that beam feels more like a cross. But there is victory on the other side, a unity and closeness that can be earned no other way.

If times are tough for you and the one you love, grit your teeth and tough it out. Bear the cross of love. The rewards are great.

The course of true love
never did run smooth.

William Shakespeare

In dreams and in love there are
no impossibilities.

Janos Arnay

How many times have I told you I hated you
and believed it in my heart? How many times
have you said you were sick and tired of me,
that we were all washed up? How many times
have we had to fall in love all over again?
Myrna Loy,
The Best Years of Our Lives

Though weary, love is not tired;
Though pressed, it is not straitened;
Though alarmed, it is not confounded.
Love securely passes through all.

Thomas à Kempis

Love is hope where reason would despair.

George, Lord Lyttleton

Be happy, because love gives us hope;
be patient in times of trouble, keep on wanting
the victory of love.

Paul of Tarsus

Love can find a way.

Ancient Proverb

There is but one genuine love potion —
consideration.

Menander

Our painful past experiences can ripen
into deep wisdom.

Shakti Gawain

Love doesn't just sit there, like stone; it has to be made, like bread, remade all the time, made anew.

Ursula K. Le Guin

Love is Forever

Luckily, I had a focus. I married. I had a family,
I never divorced. I always thought when you
married it was for life. You had to stick with it
and be brave and cope with the problems.

C.Z. Guest

When love reigns, the impossible
may be attained.

Indian proverb

Within its cage, the enlightened spirit
can sing with open throat.

Irving Singer

Ah! when will this long weary day have end,
And lend me leave to come unto my love?

Edmund Spenser

I had a lot of healing to do before I could
begin to love someone out of wholeness
and not emptiness.

Joan Oliver Goldsmith

If you are cold at night, let the promise
of my love cover you like a warm blanket.

Matthew White

Amorousness as well as grief can bring tears
to the eyes.

C.S. Lewis

The deeper that sadness carves into your
being, the more joy you can contain.

Kahlil Gibran,
The Prophet

Just as we can enjoy a
sunny day and a stormy
day in different ways,
we can learn to find
the beauty in joy and
in sadness.

Shakti Gawain

I believe that if I should die, and you were to walk near my grave, from the very depths of the earth I would hear your footsteps.

Benito Perez Galdos

Chapter 9

Love Is Forever

My father, John Cooper, died a long, slow death. For eight years his wonderful light gradually dimmed until it passed from this world. I watched in wonder as my mother cared for him those long, painful years, particularly in the end, when she held his hand at his bedside and sang to him. My father's deepest concern as he lay dying was for my mother: he grieved knowing that he had to leave her. She loves him still, and I believe that he loves her from his grave. It was witnessing the devotion of my parents to each other that convinced me that love does indeed last forever.

Love is unfathomable, miraculous, and mysterious. In the words of Rosemary Haughton, "There can be no last word on such a subject, but only a lifelong deepening of experience and understanding of love…"

True love doesn't have a happy ending;
  true love doesn't have an ending.

Unknown

If a thing loves, it is infinite.

William Blake

Love may not last forever but it lingers.

Robert Fulghum

I love thee with the breath, smiles,
  tears of all my life.

Elizabeth Barrett Browning,
to Robert Browning
Sonnets from the Portuguese

All desire wishes for eternity...
  deep, deep eternity.

Nietzsche

The world will always welcome lovers,
As time goes by.

Herman Hupfeld,
© 1931, Warner Bros. Music Corp

How vast a memory has love!

Alexander Pope

Love is a fabric which never fades,
no matter how often it is washed in the waters
of adversity and grief.

Anonymous

Love is the best thing in the world,
and the thing that lives longest.

Henry Van Dyke

Dear Joe,
If I can only succeed in making
you happy, I will have succeeded
in the biggest and most difficult
thing there is — that is, to make
one person completely happy.
Your happiness means
my happiness, and...

Marilyn Monroe,
her unfinished letter to Joe DiMaggio
the day she died.

For those who love…time is eternity….

Henry Van Dyke

Love is the only gold.

Alfred, Lord Tennyson

Some romantics think their oneness will
even outlive death, either as a renewal of the
love they attain on earth or as its perfection in
the next world….This presupposes that true
love is really indestructible. In that event, the
unity that defines romantic love can surmount
death and go on forever.

Irving Singer

And I would hear yet once before I perish
The voice which was my music —
Speak to me!

Lord Byron

Each day I love you more,
Today more than yesterday
and less than tomorrow.

Rosemonde Gerard

As we want to believe we have a permanent home in the universe, so too do we yearn for permanent oneness with some other person.

Irving Singer

"Many waters cannot quench love,"
she whispered. "Neither can the floods
drown it."

Madeleine L'Engle,
Many Waters

Not one day has passed that I have not loved you, not one night that I have not clasped you in my arms.

Napoleon,
to Josephine

But true love is a durable fire,
    In the mind ever burning,
  Never sick, never old, never dead,
    From itself never turning.

Sir Walter Raleigh

Love is never final — there's always a sequel
or the hope for one.

Robert Fulghum

Come, let us make love deathless,
              thou and I.

Herbert Trench

But love me for love's sake, that evermore
Thou mayst love on, through love's eternity.

Elizabeth Barrett Browning

Love is as strong as death.

Song of Solomon 8:6

When first you entered my room, you never went away from me.

Elizabeth Barrett Browning
to Robert Browning

Bibliography
and Index

Allende, Isabel. Aphrodite: A Memoir of the Senses. New York: HarperFlamingo, 1998.

Anand, Mulk Raj and Lance Dane, Ed. Kama Sutra of Vatsyayana. New Delhi: Arnold-Heinemann Publishers, 1982.

Boone, Gary N. On Beauty and Love. Online. BLomand. Available: www.gatech.edu/grads/b/Gary.N.Boone/beauty_and_love.html. 15 Aug 1998.

Branyon, Richard A., Ed. Italian Love. New York: Hippocrene Books, 1995.

Brümmer, Vincent. The Model of Love. Cambridge, Great Britain: Cambridge University Press, 1993.

Colman, Arthur D. and Libby Lee. Love and Ecstasy. New York: The Seabury Press, 1975.

Ewart, Andrew. The Great Lovers. New York: Hart Publishing Company, Inc., 1968.

Fulghum, Robert. True Love. New York: HarperCollins, 1997.

Gawain, Shakti. The Four Levels of Healing. Mill Valley, CA: Nataraj Publishing, 1997.

Grabowski, Michele. Pages of Romance. Online. BLomand. Available: www.geocities.com/Paris/Metro/5293/quotes.html. 17 Aug 1998.

Gray, John, Ph.D. Mars and Venus in Love. New York: HarperCollins Publishers, Inc., 1996.

Green, Jonathan, compiled by. Morrow's International Dictionary of Contemporary Quotations. New York: William Morrow & Co., Inc., 1982.

Guest, Edgar A. A Heap O' Livin'. Chicago: The Reilly & Lee Co., 1916.

Haughton, Rosemary. Love. London: C.A. Watts & Co. Ltd., 1970.

Heller, Mary Jo, selected by. I Thee Wed. Kansas City: Hallmark Editions, 1969.

Kuriansky, Dr. Judy. The Complete Idiot's Guide to a
    Healthy Relationship. New York: Alpha Books, 1998.
Lewis, C.S. The Four Loves. New York: Harcourt, Brace
    and Company, 1960.
Lindemeyer, Nancy, Ed. Victoria The Romantic Heart.
    New York: Hearst Books, 1995.
Mascetti, Manuela Dunn. The Song of Eve. New York:
    Simon & Schuster Inc., 1990.
Mason, Carl P., selected by. Great Love Scenes from
    Famous Novels. New York: The New Home Library,
    1942.
Moore, Thomas. Soul Mates. New York: HarperCollins
    Publishers, 1994.
Nin, Anaïs. Delta of Venus, Little Birds. New York:
    Harcourt Brace, 1969, 1979.
Osborne, Catherine. Eros Unveiled. Oxford: Clarendon
    Press, 1996.
Pearsall, Paul. The Ten Laws of Lasting Love. New York:
    Simon & Schuster, 1993.
Porter, Melinda Camber. The Art of Love. New York:
    Readers and Writers Publishing, 1993.
Runyeon, Richard and Carole. Creating a Life-Long Love
    Relationship. Nashville: Grace Matters Publishing,
    1997.
Singer, Irving. The Pursuit of Love. Baltimore and
    London: The Johns Hopkins University Press, 1994.
Von Kruger, Crystal and Paul Packer. Crystal's Pages of
    Romance. Online. BLomand. Available:
    www.ifb.co.uk/~failte/. 20 Aug 1998.
Walsch, Neale Donald. Conversations with God · an
    uncommon dialogue · Book 1. Charlottesville, VA:
    Hampton Roads Publishing Company, Inc., 1995.

About the Authors

Alan Ross is a writer and sports historian, with feature-story credits that include *The Sporting News*, *Lindy's Pro Football*, *Athlon Pro Football*, *NFL Insider* and *Track Record* magazine. He is also the history columnist for *Oilers Exclusive*, the official publication of the NFL's Tennessee Oilers. Ross has written four books on sports history for Walnut Grove Press. *Love Is Forever* is his first non-sports book.

Karol Cooper is a photographer, writer, and artisan living in Monteagle, Tennessee, with her husband Alan. She studied photography and design at Nashville State. Her work has appeared in national magazines and on music CD and cassette covers. She is the proud mother of three sons, Ben, Jacob and Zach. *Love Is Forever* is her first book.

For information about books from Walnut Grove Press, call 1-800-256-8584.